Great Women in History

Jane Goodall

by Erin Edison

Consulting Editor: Gail Saunders-Smith, PhD

CAPSTONE PRESS
a capstone imprint

Pebble Books are published by Capstone Press,
1710 Roe Crest Drive, North Mankato, Minnesota 56003.
www.capstonepub.com

Library of Congress Cataloging-in-Publication Data
Cataloging-in-Publication information is on file with the Library of Congress.
ISBN 978-1-4765-0143-7 (library binding)
ISBN 978-1-4765-0144-4 (paperback)
ISBN 978-1-4765-1628-8 (eBook PDF)

Note to Parents and Teachers

The Great Women in History set supports national social studies
standards related to people and culture. This book describes and
illustrates Jane Goodall. The images support early readers in
understanding the text. The repetition of words and phrases helps
early readers learn new words. This book also introduces early
readers to subject-specific vocabulary words, which are defined
in the Glossary section. Early readers may need assistance to read
some words and to use the Table of Contents, Glossary, Read More,
Internet Sites, and Index sections of the book.

Printed in the United States of America in Stevens Point, Wisconsin.
092012   006937WZS13F

Table of Contents

1934

born

Early Life

Scientist Jane Goodall has spent her life working with animals. Jane was born April 3, 1934, in London, England. Her parents were Mortimer and Margaret "Vanne" Morris Goodall. In 1938 Jane's sister, Judy, was born.

Young Jane received a toy chimpanzee from her father.

1934

born

Jane liked to learn about animals. She read books and visited zoos. Her favorite books were *The Story of Doctor Dolittle* and *Tarzan of the Apes*. After reading these stories, Jane knew she would someday go to Africa.

1934

born

1952

graduates from
high school

1957

goes to
Africa

Young Adult

Jane finished high school in 1952. Then she trained to be a secretary. Her mother told Jane she could work anywhere in the world as a secretary. In 1957 Jane traveled to Africa.

1934 — born

1952 — graduates from high school

1957 — goes to Africa

In Africa, Jane met famous scientist Dr. Louis Leakey. Jane told him about her interest in African animals. He asked Jane to work with him. Dr. Leakey wanted Jane to study chimpanzees in the wild.

1934
born

1952
graduates from
high school

1957
goes to
Africa

1960
begins work with
chimpanzees

Life's Work

In 1960 Jane arrived at Gombe
Stream Reserve in East Africa.
At first the chimpanzees wouldn't
let Jane near them. Jane sat on
a rocky hill above the chimps.
She wrote down everything she saw.

1934
born

1952
graduates from
high school

1957
goes to
Africa

1960
begins work with
chimpanzees

Over time the chimpanzees began to trust Jane. They let her sit among them. Jane saw chimps being kind to each other. But she also saw them get angry and fight. Jane was one of the first people to learn that chimpanzees make and use tools.

1934
born

1952
graduates from
high school

1957
goes to
Africa

1960
begins work with
chimpanzees

16

Jane took a break to go to college in 1962. She returned to Africa in 1965. Jane wrote about everything she learned while watching the chimpanzees. Soon people all over the world knew about Jane's amazing work.

1962

goes to college

1934
born

1952
graduates from high school

1957
goes to Africa

1960
begins work with chimpanzees

Work Continues

In 1977 Jane started the Jane Goodall Institute. Its goal is to help animals, people, and the environment.

She also has written many books about her life. In 2002 Jane was named the United Nations Messenger of Peace.

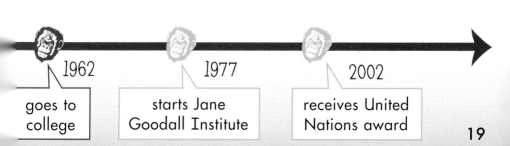

1962
goes to college

1977
starts Jane Goodall Institute

2002
receives United Nations award

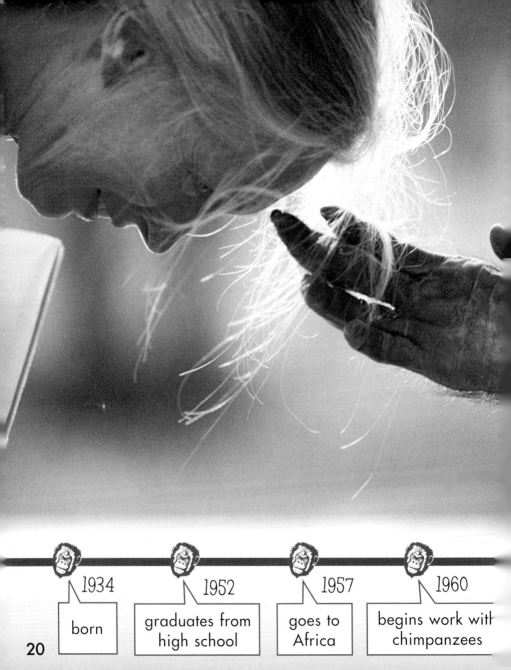

1934 — born

1952 — graduates from high school

1957 — goes to Africa

1960 — begins work with chimpanzees

Jane has studied animals for more than 50 years. Jane shares her love of chimpanzees by speaking to people around the world. She works for peace and the good treatment of all animals.

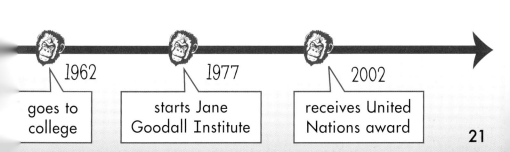

1962 — goes to college

1977 — starts Jane Goodall Institute

2002 — receives United Nations award

Glossary

college—a school students attend after high school

environment—the air, water, trees, and other natural surroundings

institute—a group that is set up to protect animals, people, and other causes

reserve—land that is protected so that animals can live there safely

scientist—a person who studies the world around us

secretary—a person who does office work

United Nations—a group of countries that works together for peace and safety

Read More

Lindeen, Mary. *Jane Goodall: Friend of the Apes.* Beginner Biographies. Edina, Minn.: Magic Wagon, 2009.

McDonnell, Patrick. *Me ... Jane.* New York: Little, Brown, 2011.

Winter, Jeanette. *The Watcher: Jane Goodall's Life with the Chimps.* New York: Schwartz & Wade Books, 2011.

Internet Sites

FactHound offers a safe, fun way to find Internet sites related to this book. All of the sites on FactHound have been researched by our staff.

Here's all you do:

Visit *www.facthound.com*

Type in this code: 9781476501437

Check out projects, games and lots more at
www.capstonekids.com

Index

Word Count: 330
Grade: 1
Early-Intervention Level: 24

Editorial Credits
Erika L. Shores, editor; Alison Thiele, designer; Wanda Winch, media researcher; Jennifer Walker, production specialist

Photo Credits
Alamy: ZUMA Wire Service, cover; Courtesy of the Jane Goodall Institute, 4, 6, 8, 10, 12, 14; iStockphoto Inc: GYI NSEA, 1; Landov: CBS, 16; National Geographic Stock: Michael Nichols, 20; Newscom: AFP/Henny Ray Abrams, 18; Shutterstock: Yury Mansiliuya, primate design element